Ringing Radiance

Devi Nangrani

Setu Publications
PITTSBURGH, USA

Ringing Radiance

By

Devi Nangrani

Setu Publications

*** Pittsburgh, PA (USA) ***

ISBN-13 (paperback): 978-1-947403-12-3

Distributed to the book trade worldwide by Setu Publications, Pittsburgh (USA)

We would be pleased to receive email correspondence regarding this publication or related topics at setuedit@gmail.com.

Setu

Setu Publications, USA

DEDICATION

At the Radiant Feet of My Master
The Ever-flowing fountain of love
That satisfies my unquenched thirst
Of expressing my gratitude for life
The greatest boon to Live from dawn to dusk

To
The soldiers of our land
Who risk their lives to save us
Protecting our borders and safeguarding us,

The doctors, the nurses, the police, the educators,
The food providers serving humanity
All through this pandemic
And to those who live in Deeds

Oh Death!
Where is thy sting?
Where do I visualize thee?
Oh! It is in my own home
In my bleeding heart
Where I see it with endless agony
For those droplets of blood
Laid in service of the Nation.
Saluting the Saviors of the Soil.

In the Garden of Love

Poetry

Flows from a Longing Heart

Contents

DEDICATION 5
Introduction 11
My Poetic Journey 12
Foreword 15
Metaphysical Verse 19
Appreciation 24
Poetry as distillation of life experiences 26
The music of my heart 28
Life is a Gift 29
Journey 30
The Source 31
Faith 32
Lighthouse 33
The Light 34
The Lost City 35
Life 36
The Lost Sheep 37
A Moment, a Lifetime 38
Oasis 39
Tide of the Mind 40
Crying Melody 41
Discovery 42
Helplessness 43
Request to the Mind 44
The Spirit 45
The Eternal Entity 46
Will of the Lord 47
Ringing Radiance 48
Grant me the Boon 49
Gift of Word 50
Our Redeemer 51
The Human Idol 52

Hide and Seek 53
Best of All 54
Demanding 55
Divine Prayer 56
Mirage and its Replica 57
The Call of the Cuckoo 58
Truth Within 59
Thoughts are Clouds 60
Sanctuary 61
The Black Sheep 62
A Bud 63
You and Only You 64
Fountain of Love 65
Cry of the Soul 66
Mercy of the Lord 67
Death a Defined Cancer 68
Truth of Life 70
The Search 71
The Living Church 72
Life and Death 73
Unheard Melody 74
A new concept of life 75
A process of recycling 76
A new reset of the creation 77
Nature is singing 78
Wants and Wishes 79
Today & Tomorrow 80
Lead and Follow 81
Thirst 82
Memories 83
This moment 84
The Will 85
The Key 86
The mirror and me 87
Foundation 88
The power of unseen 89
Images (Micro Poems) 90
Experts' Views 93
Poetry of Hope 93
The Affirming Poetics 96

In Quest …………………………………………… 99
On this journey of Inner Adventure 100
A Journey from Birth 101
On the shore of Sand 103
Author's Bio-Data.. 104
About Setu Publications............................... 108

Introduction

A lone traveler, who knows all her ways and does not restrict herself to a particular way, as it confines her and limits her ability to expand the horizon of the readers, Devi Nangrani is a unique writer and poetess in the true sense of the word - she teaches, writes, edits, translates, reviews, and is always ready to help all aspiring writers.

While her works in Sindhi language are truly incomparable, her writings in English and Hindi are equally impressive and heart-warming. During her brief career, she has been a prolific writer, churning out stories, poems, translations, and reviews. Each of her writings brings out her best.

Owing to her deep understanding of human emotions and her innate ability to choose the right set of words to express these, she finds great admiration amongst readers from different backgrounds spread over several countries. She is the winner of many literary awards.

The present collection of poems comes from her earlier writings scattered on different writing and poetry platforms. This is the first attempt of putting together all her earlier poems in the present book 'Ringing Radiance.'

Raja Sharma
A professor of Physics and English
Currently a resident of Nepal.

My Poetic Journey

In the flow and flaw of the magnificent language
What I feel...
Why I feel...
On the wings of Poetry
I flutter and fly like a butterfly
To see the beauty that surrounds me
In its utmost softness of silk
To feel the tenderness of ecstasy

Poetry is nothing but language of the heart. Every person who can think logically and listen to the heartbeat can emotionally express feelings of love, hate, compassion, anger, feel and hurt balance system.

Writing poetry is like nourishing a garden where we sow seeds of thoughts, which sprout with the input of efforts when nourished with attentive seasoning. It is only then that the colorful ideas blossom with fragrance. The sown speechless thoughts take the support of words to find expression, they grow and mature as saplings, start whispering and walking. Still the fact remains unchanged that 'Life' is poetry' but poetry is not life.' Words and poet have a co-relative bond. Words may exist without a writer, but a writer cannot exist without words. Poetry in form of words on paper is nothing but the fruit of thoughts that can find expression in the flow and flaw of the language of the heart.

Every person is a born talented artist. One being a painter, other being a journalist, yet another, a sculptor and the next one a poet. The sculptor chips the hard rock and turns it in fertile model of his imagination, carving to the finest core of the hardened rock to replicate tenderness and beauty. An artist uses rainbow colors to bring to life the characters that he imagines to be breathing on his canvas. Similarly, a poet uses fine words with or without rhyme and rhythm to express his own feelings. In a way a poet's imagination through words begins to breathe, creep, dance, and flutter like a butterfly so that it can rhyme with nature that is so beautiful, so lively and so unique, where the thought are so beautifully woven in a majestic flow of ripples-

Like a grand river of light
Flowing from
A needle's orifice

For me poetry is another name for the encounter of self with both the worlds, the inner and outer, in a way the world and the word reflect each other. The thoughts stir within like the current of events enforcing the words to find existence in expression. There is a turmoil of the flow of the unknown source yet to be explored and experienced like a river flowing within. The expression in words finds meaning through the prism of a poem. It is here that my joys and sorrows, my passions and thoughts, my failures and attainments, my downfalls and elevations find solace in that beam of fluorescence and indeed the unknown mysteries expose as the ray of light emerging from darkness.

This expression of thoughts in words is like connecting to self to the core of the very being. It is here that I feel and believe that poetry is a gift of God:
Poetry is a gift from God.

Specially for me to be with self
Never to be alone, never to be lonely
It is my friend for all times
In joy or sorrow
Today and tomorrow
In joy, it flies with me
Across the kaleidoscopic horizon
Sailing on the ocean of light.
In sorrow, it sinks with me
In the depths of darkness.
And it is here, only here
I find light in darkness.
I am never alone now,
For, poetry is with me.
It is my all-time companion
My soul mate like God.

Devi Nangrani
New Jersey

Foreword

My joy knew no bounds when the distinguished poet Devi Nangrani ji approached me for a foreword for her poetry collection "Ringing Radiance," after a well-wisher had referred my name. Devi Nangrani is a committed educator, multilingual, prolific writer with over forty books to her credit, and a versatile personality; despite her accomplishments, I found her endearing during the tête-à-tête we had over a WhatsApp call. Her voice rings with radiance!

'Ringing Radiance' the title of her new collection of sixty-two poems reveals varied thoughts in unison - self-awareness, self-exploration, and self-discovery leading to love, understanding and acceptance of the flow of the cosmos. It is a compilation of poems written over a period of time. Devi Nangrani has meticulously collated the lyrics (verse libre) for poetry lovers to rejoice and appreciate the higher purpose of human existence. The poems blossom in the path of attached detachment, without letting the chaos of the world rule the mind: "I am the singing melody of my Land/ That gently tunes in rhythm..." (The music of my heart)

As an ardent seeker, the poet upholds that the purpose of human life is not merely to enjoy sense pleasures and procreation as humans alone are endowed with discriminatory thinking to understand the 'God' within, which has been revealed with great clarity for the realization of self from within."
"If/ You look beyond with eyes of faith
You recover from blindness that blinds. (Faith)"

These lines serve as balm in today's existential reality that has left Man with growing fear and uncertainty.

A deep understanding of life and death is revealed in the poem 'Light.' Acceptance of both life and death in the process of evolution and talking about it as 'not been extinguished, it is in the hearts of humans.' The subsequent verse, 'Life' further discloses the equanimity of the poet's mind in these lines-
'May be only this moment / This unit of life/ Is our treasure!'

'In A Moment, A Lifetime,' the poet subtly brings out the vices of the human mind: 'A passion to want more and more' and ending the verse with the direct pointer - 'the span of life, a limited span.' In the 'Oasis,' of existence, she pleads that the 'dark soul be atoned by redemption,' while in the 'Tide of the mind' she resigns to the fact that everything goes back to its origin:
"Come I may but go I must/ To fulfill nature's perfect plan.

The quest reveals another layer when it leads to the desire to be freed from the cycle of births and death- "Again let me not enter a woman's womb" (Discovery). In these lines, the poet echoes the profound truths of the cyclical process of life and death as expounded by the great saint- philosopher Adi Shankara: 'punarapi janani jathare sayanam.'

The 'realization' rings with radiance when the truth dawns-
"Only now I have realized that you are Effulgence,
That you are the "Lord of Lords" (Ringing Radiance).

The verses continue with the 'yearning to see a glimpse' fully conscious that she knows 'nothing' and the learning is 'ever-failing.' Talking of life as 'coin with two phases' the poet emphasizes: 'Live it to the fullest but mourn not.'. The mention of 'cuckoo' instantly flashes William Wordsworth's immortal lines:

"O Cuckoo! shall I call thee Bird,
Or but a wandering Voice?"

The Romantic poet joyfully addresses the cuckoo as 'Blithe New Comer." Contrastingly, Devi Nangrani's "Call of the cuckoo/ Has pain in the pitch. It is the soaring cry/ Of the longing heart." In 'Truth Within' the poet describes the moment of bliss as an 'unbelievable' treasure, whose 'sights was blinding/unfolding the light in darkness.' Engulfed in the dazzling brilliance, 'the unspoken words fail to talk.' Duality gone; the Oneness left!

A poignant and powerful poem is 'Death a Defined Cancer' where the poet poses several questions: 'What is this pattern of life? The life we live,/ When we really live./ Is it when we are alive?/ Or, when we pass away?'
The answers to these evident questions are revealed by the poet in 'Truth of Life': 'The last day, terrible & frightful/ Everyone around you will speak/ But you will remain silent.' The mystical experiences are further highlighted in 'Life and Death': The light that vanishes,/The life that is extinguished,/Shall not go beyond the graves,/For it was never ever born,/Nor did it fade.

Taking a deviation from the mystical experiences, the poet brings in the truths of worldly life in 'The Will.'

'Tomorrow you will be governed/ At this very place, a new history will be written/ Tomorrow your successors will sign themselves, /Without acknowledging your wants and wishes/ Where I am signing today.'

What a profound philosophy expressed here! The occurrences of today becomes history tomorrow.

The poet's voice roars with deep understanding and conviction in 'The Key.'-

'If you think you shall stem me/ with the shackles of your sweet selfish love/you are mistaken.'

Rejuvenation, cyclical changes, creation, destruction, creation again - profound insights about that Immortal One in this mortal world afflicted with pain, sorrows and uncertainties has been the poet's sheath as she claims-

Reality survives
All dreams come to an end
When I awake

This micro poem brings to mind Henry David Thoreau's famous quote- "Only that day dawns to which we are awake." In simple words, only one who is awake sees the rising sun. As the rising sun brings in hope and optimism, 'Ringing Radiance' is certain to offer solace to individuals trapped in mundane existence, to recognize that love, compassion, patience, surrender, humility and discrimination comprise the primary aspects of liberation and peace. This collection is certain to evoke positivity in many hearts.

Hema Ravi

Celebrated author of 'Everyday English,' 'Write Right Handwriting Series 1,2,3,' co-author of Sing Along Indian Rhymes' and 'Everyday Hindi.' Editor (Efflorescence) and is the Secretary of the Chennai Poets' Circle, Chennai. Hemaravi24@gmail.com

Metaphysical Verse

Devi Nangrani's metaphysical verse adorns the pages of her new book titled RINGING RADIANCE which echoes both her literary expression and her philosophical reflections. Her poems have the tenderness and mellifluity of a breeze that opens doors and windows into a garden permeated with the presence of the Divine. At the same time, they have the vitality and clarity of diamonds found in nature. The fusing of these two dimensions constitutes the body and soul of her poetry. RINGING RADIANCE is a synthesis of her inner and outer light that encompasses the whole framework of human life seeking a relationship with the universe. The struggle to establish such a satisfying and dynamic relationship began with the first human being and continues to haunt humanity. That struggle is perhaps the force that moves the universe and its denizens to horizontal and vertical movement, physical as well as intellectual.

Given the advances in knowledge and in technological prowess, one sees in modern times that large populations look for solace in worldly progress and its diversions, setting aside aspirations of spiritual growth. Contemporary literature, especially poetry, has captured the human predicament of seeking bliss in the transient and physical dimensions of life in the universe.

It requires great courage today for a feeling and thinking practitioner of art to go beyond the spatial and the temporal and to tap the physical, mental and spiritual dimensions gifted to human beings. Devi Nangrani brings to bear a sense of consistency and seriousness to the struggle to revisit fundamental themes connecting human consciousness to the magic, mystery and metaphysical grandeur of Divine-human relationship.

She is a Promethean figure who believes, not in nostalgia but in a creative search to address a number of themes: inner/outer, reality/appearance, mind/matter, and body/soul. All these themes in her hands become oars to undertake a journey in the ocean of light. This is a journey of the heart — neither inner nor outer but holistic; of a Reality which is neither here nor there but everywhere; of a soul that is not apart from mind and matter but suffusing both and even extending beyond; and of creative possibilities in which worldly icons and landmarks are no longer ends n themselves but steps in an unending journey embracing both life and death.

Devi Nangrani's conclusions about the Divine-human relationship are a model of clarity and conviction. For her, religions mean nothing if they are not steppingstones in the journey of love. Life and the universe are not to be treated lightly as disposable entities. All glow in the Divine light and have to be treated as paths leading to the Divine. For her, the door to the divine garden runs through the human heart.

In this framework, Devi Nangrani's poems are spiritual utterances providing a glimpse of her spiritual adventure with its trials and tribulations, as well as the experience of receiving light and wisdom. Let us refer to some poems which illustrate her approach to life as well as art. Poetry for her has a divine purpose: 'to mingle/my voice in the vibrations/ which is a part of the Eternal Music.' The heart is central to her work. 'Listen to my heartbeat', she says in *The News of my Heart*. 'I am the singing melody of my Lord '. Life for her is a gift to undertake 'a search for the self' by awakening from 'spiritual slumber ' to 'self-realisation '. She likens the self's blossoming to mushrooms 'that know not but growth'. She regards life's journey as both 'physical and astral'. She compares her 'real self' to an 'island/hidden in the sea of my body/ in there I shed a tear'. The journey of life and self becomes fruitful when, sublimating pain and misery, or 'the hide and seek', she seeks 'to free myself/From my own web' and resolves to 'retrace and go back to the Source'.

Human knowledge in this framework is not dependent on the mind and reason alone. Faith too is a source of experience and knowledge:
If/you look beyond with eyes of faith/ You recover from blindness that blends. She sums up her thoughts in the poem FAITH as follows: 'See with the eyes of faith/ Feel with heart full of faith/ That God is working in your life...'.

Her symbol for life's wisdom is the flow and glow of light experienced by a seeker. 'Create your own lighthouse', she says, 'The powerhouse of radiance/That can be the Guide'. These lines express her courage to be and the resolve to become. They also reflect her fiercely independent spirit rooted in creativity and self-discovery. 'Light', she wrote is 'in us, within us, around us/Forever till Eternity'.

It is not possible to illustrate her variegated but inter-related themes comprehensively in this essay. However,

I invite the reader's attention to the following poems to gain a bird's eye view of the intellectual and spiritual space covered by her poetic imagination: *A Moment, a Lifetime; Oneness; Oasis; Tale of the Mind; Cry of the Soul; Life and Death; Discovery;* and *Thirst.*

Let me conclude by saying that I consider myself a fellow traveller and pilgrim with Devi Nangrani to the Sanctuary of the Divine. Some of her poems usher me into God's presence on the wings of a transparent faith of the universe and life as God's own creation. Both of us believe that the beating, feeling, thinking Body - Mind - Soul - Heart combination is a divine miracle. Faith in this miracle grows with every poem found in this book. Here are a few examples:

To
Reproduce his radiance within us
Experience his presence in us
To
Believe that he is with us
Today and always
(Demanding)

O Divine Lord
It is from ye and only ye
Comes the light....
(Divine Prayer)

You are my only escort, oh omnipotent Lord.
(Our Redeemer)

How ignorant of me, Oh Lord transcendental
That I have been rambling only along the shore
What kept me yonder from Thee...

(Gift of the Word)

Only now I have realised
That you are effulgence.
(Ringing Radiance)

And finally, a master poem which is a fervent prayer for wisdom to recognise the Divine:
Oh Lord,
Give me the insight
So I remember you
I see you, adore you, love you
Worship you the way you want...
(The Call of the Cuckoo)

To sum up, this entire book by the thoughtful expression of the poet is inundated by the flood of divine consciousness and an abiding faith in His miracles of life and the universe.

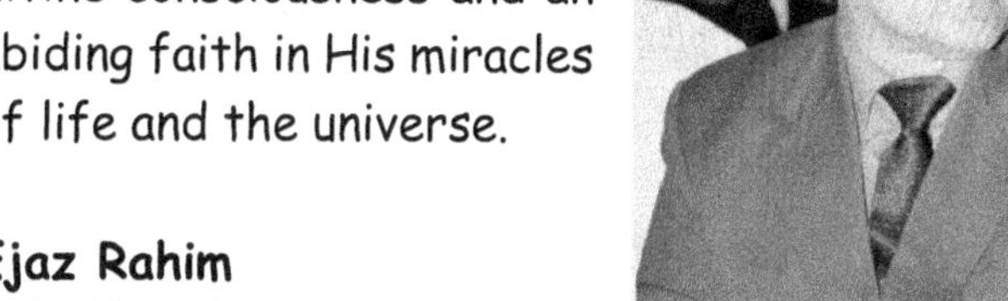

Ejaz Rahim
Retired from Government service in 2006, Awarded Honorary Doctorate of Letters by the Metropolitan University of Dublin in 2009, is a living legend from the soil of Sindh.
ejaz.rahim@hotmail.com

Appreciation

On Water and Togetherness

There's an old apocryphal adage that the Chinese symbol for "poetry" is a combination of the Chinese characters for "word" and "temple." This thought kept poking at the back of my mind as I navigated these pages. There is a wonderful togetherness that radiates throughout these poems. In the age of individualism and selfishness, it's important to pull yourself back into the world around you "and merge this 'drop' in your gracious ocean," as Nangrani writes in "Grant me the Boon." Speaking of water, I would be remiss if I did not call attention to the wonderful tropes surrounding water and the sea in *Ringing Radiance* (the word "ocean" appears 11 times, "water" 14 times, and "drop" 12 times throughout the text). "My mind is a sandy particle / With unquenched thirst" she writes in "Thirst," and indeed, is there not an infinite thirst inside all of us? Water is constantly in motion. Streams, rivers, and tides are always in motion, and those little particles of water never return to their previous location. They move forward, and they never revisit their past. So why do we?

Often, we find ourselves locked into our obsessions, goals, and progress. We fixate over the next thing we want to buy, the next place we want to go, and where that next rush of satisfaction will come from. All eyes remain fixed on the destination. We are ships sailing rough waters—binoculars out, scanning the horizon for that little point of light that will guide us to the thing we want. But if a ship is even one degree off-course, it will end up in a completely different location. I think we all know this, and even the most rigorous of psychologists will acknowledge that this fear underlines our deepest motivations and insecurities. What if this new car won't make me happy? What if this shirt makes me look fat? What if I should ask for a raise before my next performance review? Nangrani's work here reminds us that when we fixate ourselves on the horizon—when we obsess over what's next—we forget about what's actually happening on the ship. In "Lighthouse," the speaker of the poem advises you, "While in the body / Radiate as the rays do / Create your own lighthouse." We should all aspire to be water. To let go of the past and be present in our own bodies. Nangrani offers a blueprint here. Allow yourself to tune in to a higher frequency and meet yourself on your own terms: for God, for your own well-being, and for all of the joys that surround you.

Stay hydrated, my dear friends.

Eric McClure

Former teacher of English, published poet, and author,
was the winner of the Paul Carroll award for outstanding achievement in creative writing at the University of Illinois at Chicago.
etmcclure91@gmail.com.

Poetry as distillation of life experiences

Poets are a strange clan of misfits. They are hopeless romantics with a dreamy perspective on life. They use poetry introspectively as a mirror to reveal unpleasant truths subtly while using words as balm to soothe the troubled soul; they are creators who chart their own unconventional path. Since this book celebrates the work of one such poet, it is only apt that I am writing few words on this book -Devi Maasi, as I call Devi Nangrani ji (as she is my aunt) has played an important role in my life, notwithstanding her personal struggles to make a mark for herself in the Western world. Although, I have been raised in the West, I still cherish and appreciate Indian languages, the poetry, the art, culture and the multi-diversity of the ethnic land- India.

In my younger years, I used to think that poetry is just flowery language. I thought poets only need flair and mastery over the language and the poetry just flows. I couldn't have been more incorrect. Over the years, I have realized that good poetry is often a highly concentrated distillate of one's life experiences, both positive and negative.

There is a certain *je ne sais quoi* about her compared to other ladies of that time. Despite the setbacks in her life, she persevered and evolved into a multi-faceted and confident woman - a teacher, an author with 40 books to her name, a multilingual poet (she writes in English, Hindi, Urdu, Sindhi) with a solid understanding of Hindustani classical music. Some of these disciplines are inter-related - eg, a grounding in the *raag/taal* framework of Hindustani classical music is necessary to write Urdu poetry such as *ghazals*. This interdisciplinary approach to her craft makes Devi *Maasi's* contributions even more commendable.

Whenever I read Devi *Maasi's* poetry, I see a distillation of life experiences that shaped her. I hope your experience of reading this poetic compilation is as pleasurable as mine - introspective, poignant and joyous - a cocktail of emotions!

Vinay Athma

A resident of California, engineer by profession, currently working for Amazon, building technology products.

vinay_athma@yahoo.com

The music of my heart

Listen to my Heartbeat
I am the singing melody of my Land
That gently tunes in rhythm
Wrapping me in her essence.
My thoughts dance in tune
With the melody of my heartbeat
In the Canopy of fragrance
They dance as daisies in my memory
Growing with me where I stand
Sometimes longer, at times shorter
But never have I felt without the Source
That reflects my thoughts
To dance with the melody
Of my Heartbeat.

Life is a Gift

Wait not for the tides to subside in the ocean
Wait not for the symptoms of old age or wisdom
To knock you with a shock

That life is a phantom
Wait not for the ailments of the heart or head
To obstruct thy search for search of the 'self'
Wait not for the miracle to awaken thy slumber
A spiritual slumber That sleeps in a dark chamber
Wait not for the desire to dwindle or dry
For mushrooms are they

That know not but growth
Wait not for the pleasure or pain of the life
To kindle thy understanding

For a knowledge of the 'self'
Life is a gift, a holy gift not for gambling
But for realization of self from within.

Journey

When I travel
From the tip of my toe to the top
With no distinction between
The physical and astral me
That is the moment of fire
Between me and my real self
To meet myself and enjoy the union.
Within me is an island
Hidden from the sea of my body
In there I shed a tear
Hidden from the eye of my spirit.
For I feel the separation
The yearning, a tearing apart void
In the space that is within me
To reach my destination
Never to be back from top to toe.

The Source

On
The wings of thought,
I, rise high and high
To See the glory of nature
In

Pleasure and paradise,
In pool of pain and misery

Where
I Wander from dawn to dusk
Wherever desire takes me
In pursuit of pleasure
To See something exciting
To See something unseen
Finally
The urge to free myself
From my own web
Compels me
To retrace and go back,
To the Source.

Faith

If
You look beyond with eyes of faith
You recover from blindness that blinds.
If
You see with eyes of faith
The unseen world within you
Opens the gates for you to a new world.
If
You see with eyes of faith
You find yourself fortified at a new level
Better off than you were before.
For
He is all-powerful Almighty God
And in control of all.
Then
You will forget all you complained
And then, You will see with eyes of faith
Feel with heart full of faith
That God is working in your life.

*

Lighthouse

The Sunset
Of life is still ahead
The receding rays
Of dusk still glow
For they are
The lighthouse of radiance
For the sinking vessels
Those come in this world
To come and go empty.

Awake Oh Soul!
While in the body
Radiate as the rays do
Create your own lighthouse
The powerhouse of radiance
That can be the guide
And the master indicator
To lead and follow without fear
To save the sinking vessel of this body.

The Light

The souls that depart
Leave the abode and merge
The source of light
To enlighten the darkness.
The saddest of the hearts
The hearts that bleed
The hearts that are agonized
For the fear that
Light has vanished.

It is a cloud,
A cloud with a silver lining
For the light that faded,
The light that vanished,
Has not been extinguished
It is in the hearts of humans,
To create the Joyous Joy,
It is in hearts to fade away agony
That is deep down in us.
To blossom as a flower from a bud.
That the Lord has sown and cherished
During his presence with us,
During his absence with us.
The abstract absence is vague,
It is a wavering unstable phase of darkness
He is light, he is the lighthouse
In us, within us, around us
Forever till Eternity.

The Lost City

The spot is vacant
In here and out there
For each one of the creation
Created by the creator
In the lost city of destination.

Here we wander
To find ourselves
In the world of chaos
Drinking the sore of pain
In search of the source.

Within the core
We find the link of silence
From it sprout the buds of True Spirit
That led us to the road of silence,
To help us discover the lost city.

Life

Life is a journey
Through rough and smooth roads
Of rise and fall of the labyrinth
Of odd and even blows of life's journey
Timely & untimely winds
It is still a span of breaths
For some years, some moments
Or
May be only this moment !
This unit of life
Is our treasure!
So treasure it every moment
As a miser does his wealth
To make life worthy!

The Lost Sheep

I am the lost sheep, I know My Lord!
You wander from heaven to hell
In search of me, to take me with you
In thine kingdom of ecstasy

I belong to thee
Do hold my hand to pull me out
Of these extrications of illusion
To cure my sick self
That longs to be with you.
I look for thee here and there, but not within Where
you dwell in me for me
More closer to me than my breaths

Still I cannot reach you, but you can
Do lead me, so I can follow you
On your footprints
To reach safely my Homeland.

A Moment, a Lifetime

A feeling of incompleteness
A passion to want more and more
To the very end of limitless boundary
Not knowing -
How much land does a man need?
To take breaths from sunrise to sunset
That is the span of life, a limited span
A moment, a lifetime.

Oasis

Oh Lord! It is only your benevolence
That I have come to your 'oasis'.

This world is full of fairs and nightmares
This mundane world knows only flashy flares.
Desert I, my life's dreary portals
To seek thine lotus petals.

'Merry go round' appears this life
There remains nothing but grief and strife.
Like the waves of the blue ocean
My mind gets tossed in thought's oscillation.
The one who teaches me wisdom is thy self
And ye remind me of the mission.

Bless me to lose my 'self' in meditation
Let my dark soul be atoned by redemption.
Let my heart be attuned to perfection
By bathing in thy Effulgent Ray diffusion.

Tide of the Mind

Have you ever seen an ocean?
It's deep blue flowing water?
The thrashing roaring waves
Arising from within the waters
The waves arising from the waves,
Coming towards the shore
And receding back in dismay.
To give the message
"Come I may; but go I must.
To fulfill nature's perfect plan."

Have you ever heard the whispering cry?
The resounding agony of the waves?

Crying Melody

Have you ever heard
The crying melody of thoughts?
When a single thought
Proceeding yet another
Clashes, cracks, breaks
Leaving the disturbed entity
To live in the cage of this body
Withering with every cry
As bleeding droplets
In complete harmony of the breaths
For the reunion.

Discovery

Oh Lord! As a babe witnessing the bulls fight,
I cry aloud in lonesome fright,
Entangled in the worldly plight
My soul is crying for the divine light.

Let my soul be tuned to divine communion
In the utmost perfection, harmony & clarion,
Again let me not enter a woman's womb,
Or trod the path that leads to the tomb.

Oh Lord! The plight of separation is a sore,
The bleeding starts at the very core.
The fire to be together intensifies
As the distance seems to never ending

Oh Lord! In the depths of sheaths I find,
Thee in the symphony of sound
As the ringing radiance makes me spellbound
I see the symbol of Prudence around.

Helplessness

The mind is in turmoil at its helplessness
The soul struggling against its helplessness
Deepening the sadness of the rebellious heart.

Worldly we inspect ourselves
We are the defendants and the judges
The self-judgment falsifies defeat and victory.

It is a helpless surrender,
We resign to our fates at one hand
And the law that governs us,
Rules helplessly at the other hand.

Request to the Mind

Oh mind! Why don't you leap forward?
As does nature that never retraces.
River flowing out of Rocky Mountains
Only leaps forward.
The rivulet of youth follows its footprints.
Time leaps forward, never retraces behind.
Life leaps forward to death.
Oh Human Mind!
Why can't you march forward?
Why do you retrace back?
Why do you break the law?
The rest of the creation never looks back?
Why do you do that?
To agonize the body
That gives you shelter?
Why? Why?

The Spirit

For whose company does the soul descend?
On this earth in every birth?
And still leap from the hearth,
To the funeral pyre,
When the inner flame leaves the mortal frame?
Who comes here?
For whose company, who knows?
Yes! Knows he, only the "Nameless HE"
'Self-born' but never forlorn:
Because of his Evolution, his Leela
Creates a wonderful revolution, his consort 'Maya'.
The only company is 'He'
The Eternal Symphony to all life.
The sixth sense is only to know
This sweet essence in this worldly strife
In fire or mire, on earth or heaven,
He is all in all.

The Eternal Entity

My Lord!
Longing and yearning for thine Darshan's feast
On the wings of thoughts, my soul flies
But, why not pity me yet my Lord!
Why no mercy on this forlorn bard?

O Lord of purity!
Why have thou come here to embrace earthly fire
As a single entity of eternal divinity?
Is it to save the ever-erring humanity?
From sham vanity and revert to immortality?

O Personified sanctity!
Without thy bountiful shower of mercy
Where will this wandering soul get any courtesy?
Long is the avenue to reach thy ecstasy,
Pray let not my sweet dream be in fantasy.

Will of the Lord

Oh Lord! Your sweet will
Is a grove of the fragrant sandal.
Whereas mine is only a vehicle
For spreading other's scandal.

My Resplendent Lord! How can
My bondage with you divine
Be forgotten by the rambling mind?

Oh Lord! Only you know
As thou are omnipresent
The secret of my turbulent heart.
You are the Eternal powerhouse
Engineering and transmitting energy
To every soul and sphere
Oh Lord! Let thy Grace
The sandal's sweet fragrance
Fill in and around me your sweet fragrance.

Ringing Radiance

I prostrate unto Thee
One who hath rendered peace unto me.

In my heart, thy compassionate voice is heard,
Oh Lord! None excels you in this world.

Unaware of you from time of my birth,
I was singing the glory of Hari, Hara and Brahma:

Only now I have realized that you are Effulgence,
That you are the "Lord of Lords"
And the Ringing Radiance.

Grant me the Boon

Grant me that only 'gain"
To merge in thy Lotus Feet again.
Am I to lament throughout the day
Or torture my 'self' for the loss of the gay?

Like the cow and its calf's desperation
My spirit is tormented with your separation.
Like a bubble in the water in this life mundane
To renounce it fully I need thy grace divine.

You are leading us from sin unto life eternal
Merciful are thou father paternal.
Our name and fame goes in the dustbin
Let my heart remain tuned to the self within.

Save me from the life that is shackled
And merge this 'drop' in your gracious ocean.

Gift of Word

How mean of me, O Lord Merciful!
To deny thee thy share, a petty one tenth a day
Where I fail; still I plod as turtle, not hare.
To reach our home divine, in thy Masterly care.

How ridiculous of me, O Lord radiant!
That I was drunk deep with the wine of polytheism!
Alas! Why did I waste those years precious?
Playing with the outer luster of the shells
And not seeking the pearl at its core.

How ignorant of me, O Lord Transcendental!
That I have been rambling only along the shore
What kept me yonder from Thee, never to ponder?
That goal of life is to dive deep and not to sink.

How uncouth of me, O my savior!
I decorate only the outskirts of Thy temple holy
And fill it within my thoughts unholy and foul
That the precious Gift of WORD lost in luster fine.

Our Redeemer

You are my only escort, oh omnipotent Lord
When I am Thine and you are mine,
Is not also this whole universe mine?
More than motherly love weighs your compassion,
When life ebbs away, you are the only escort,
To accompany and free me from *Kal's* tension.
Day by day my karma grows like a mound,
The mind in the *Maya* is bound,
Why doesn't our *karma* get nullified
Why do they get multiplied?
The illusionary *Maya* seems real,
It may not be uprooted till the mind is clear.
That Herculean feet is impossible
Unless you find a true anchor,
A genuine Guru, an eternal friend,
To free me from the shackles of the bondage,
And put an end to the cycle
Of births and deaths.

Kal = death
Maya = delusion or illusion
Karma = law of cause & effect/ web of actions

The Human Idol

The glory and grace of thine Darshan
Sparkles and spotless, is a 'Human Idol'
It would not touch wealth or valor
But will set a bound for your passions and fashions.

Behold but leave not the household
Be in the world, but not of the world
These are the showers of his grace,
Those leave no sinful trace.

Long live that Idol, my Beloved
The Idol of justice and ocean of bliss.

Hide and Seek

How graciously you have given
The Gift of thine Holy Name
And opened my latent inner shrine
To worship Radiant Divine oh Lord!

Yearning to see a glimpse of thee
Praying earnestly for your presence
Realizing that is the only solution
For the soul's final emancipation.

The mortal eyes of mine-both
Ramble about almost daily.
The wisdom eye within keeps focus
In quest of you daily.

But why is this cycle of hide and seek
With the poor soul so meek?
Has the seeking soul to weep daily
For sight of that sunshine that blinds me?

Best of All

Oh Lord!
Forgive me for what I say
For I know not what I say
Forgive me for what I hear.
For I misunderstand, and
Misinterpret what I hear.

Let the witches in me vanish
Let the ghost in me die
So that the Holy Ghost may survive.
For I know not how to thank Thee
For the daily bread that I deserve not.

I the Jack of all, knowest nothing
Thou the master, knowest all of all.
I do the best of all I know
You do the best of all for all.

Demanding

He
Who gives us life's time span,
To breathe till we die,
He
Wants us to give him time
That is timeless and undivided
To
Still and allign,
The body
The mind
The soul
To
Reproduce his radiance in us,
Experience his presence in us,
To
Believe that he is with us,
Today and always.

Divine Prayer

Oh Divine Lord!
Thine Radiant form supreme,
Leaves me amazed.
To adore thee
With all my ever-failing intelligence
To be still elevated by
Thine sole supreme power.

Oh Divine Lord!
It is from ye and only ye,
Comes the light that helps,
The emergence of brilliance,
A means to prove
That every darkest cloud,
Has a silver lining.

Mirage and its Replica

Life is a mirage beyond captivity
It is a coin with two phases
Pleasure, malice, Joy and sorrow
Good and bad, hate and love.
Live it to the fullest but mourn not.

It is a passing phase and has to pass by
Littering the world with light.
The earth, the water, the green and you
And when it does, it absorbs the warmth
Transform it in love to spread it around you.

In you is pleasure and malice, in you is joy and sorrow
In you is good and bad, hate and love
But the coin turns around changing the whole outlook.
Good dominates the bad, love overpowers hate
Joy absorbs sorrow, pleasure replaces malice
Love with multiple shades,
Makes the living mirage, a memorable replica.

The Call of the Cuckoo

The call of the cuckoo
Has pain in the pitch
It is the soaring cry
Of the longing heart.

Oh Lord!
I remember you,
But not the way you want
I see you, I adore you, I love you,
I worship you,

Oh Lord!
Give me the insight
So I remember you,
I see you, adore you, love you
Worship you, the way you want.

Truth Within

Unbelievable is the treasure I saw
It's beauty clouded my vision
The sight of sights was blinding
Unfolding the light in darkness
The unspoken words fail to talk
To describe that is more than
What we hear from the legends
From the epics that retell
The legends are old
But still, new to the seeker
He who beholds
The mind in stillness.

Thoughts are Clouds

Thoughts are like clouds,
They rise, arise, and
Drop down as melted ice.
It is nice to view, to feel the beauty
As they drop down in space
Dripping down as water drops
But when they fall
It hurts, to see them on the ground
Mingled with dust
All messed up
Like a jumble on the sands.

Thoughts are like clouds
They ought to rise, and arise
To evaporate in the sky
To be air in air, ether in ether
Like the marks of footsteps on sand.

Sanctuary

They are the lucky ones
Those have a sanctuary within
To breed on, to live on,
As does a bird on the perch of a branch.
Some have no shelter, no sanctuary
If no fate favors them.

The taste of love
Takes the hold of life
The love that takes the hold
Detaches one from all.
But, still
The thirst will remain unquenched.
Such love is unique
The lover is unique too
He gives up freedom
Accepts bondage of love
Creating a world
A web to entangle him
And let him live in a sanctuary,
Breaking the cage
Flying as a free bird
To sing on the perch
In the woods of sanctuary.
To fulfill the goal of life
In this life as humans.

The Black Sheep

Oh Gracious Lord,
Cleanse me with thy grace
As I am the black sheep
Hammering and explanations don't help me,
You are the beginning and the end of all reality.
Give me an eye
To see the glow of the emergence of light
Coming from the source, which is my destination
Give me love, that sees no gain, no securities
Just the fruit of being in thine Lotus Feet

A Bud

In the garden of my heart blooms a bud
To see the sight of sights
The never tasted purely nectar of love!
The bud had none but one
As it's sweetheart, full of brimming love
And the bud took, gay and joyous colors
Making the lovable heart, it's destination
And a place of peace, a solitary home
Here blooms the bud into a perfect flower
Nourished by the nectar of love.

You and Only You

In you is pleasure and malice,
In you is joy and sorrow.
In you is good and bad, hate and love.
But the coin turns around changing the whole outlook.
Good dominates the bad, love overpowers hate
Joy absorbs sorrow, pleasure replaces malice.

Fountain of Love

Come to me Oh Ye Lord,
The vacant heart awaits you.

Blessed is thine coming, for
It forces me to be humming
The eternal everlasting music
That leads to ecstasy.

When I tune on myself with you
The stars appear jingling on the sky blue,
The line of merriest constellation
Takes me away from desolation,
Leading to the way that leads
To the eternal everlasting bliss.

A thorough contradiction beholds life!
The life that is gone,
The life that is to come,
No regrets for the life that is gone,
But for life that's to come,

I've nothing else but to hum,
The glowing tune of life,
That echoes from the deepest core,
Still resounding more and more
Bringing back to me,
The ever-flowing fountain of love.

Cry of the Soul

The path to be trodden
Tires me to no end,
Lest assured am I
Tread I've to, go I must.
The destiny awaits me there,
Where I am destined to reach.
It is the divine power that pulls me,
To the place of eternal solace,
The place of eternal rest
The void lingers, creating the longing,
To meet my master,
The perfect One.
The vast expanse of ocean ahead,
Must absorb me in itself,
The never-ending space,
That overlaps me,
And hovers over my thoughts,
Must help me to mingle,
My voice in its vibrations,
Which is a part of the Eternal Music,
The Word.
Come I from the word,
Go I must in it.
For there is my inn,
That calls me in.
The void is filled; the journey is complete,
The Holy Spirit that echoes in me,
Resounds the truth, The Eternal truth
That calls me.

Mercy of the Lord

Bountiful is the mercy of the Lord
Bountifully he showers it no end,
The giver and the taker on par stand.
The giver gives, gives and gives
The taker, takes and takes until
He fades away
Giving place to yet another taker
And in the continuous chain
The rhythm of give and take continues
Until and unless, the taker
Stabilizes with his mercy,
Absorbing the bounty
To become free from the chain
Yes, the chain of give and take.
To merge as a drop of ocean
Losing its identity to be one with the Origin.

Death a Defined Cancer

What is this wrath?
The wrath of nature,
That falls on the flower,
That bloom not to the fullest.
What is this sting?
That pains not the soul,
But still it pains; it pains
The bodies that bind,
The attachment with the detached.
What is this pattern of life?
The life we live,
When we really live.
Is it when we are alive?
Or, when we pass away?
The soundness of the mind,
Falls a prey to the merciless wrath.
Can a victim escape,
Life or death?
We escape ourselves,
But not death!
The supreme truth of life
That we live.
The end and object of life,
We attain in death.
The soothing reality of ailing soul,
That lives today,
Shall tomorrow,
Till decades to come, till eternity.
To seek peace and solitude,
In the long lasting sleep.
Memoirs can't be buried

They go beyond the grave,
The grave that covers the body,
The grave that covers the soul.
But does it?
No, it lingers around
A'dmist the memoirs
That are living,
That never die.

Truth of Life

Try to bring to your mind
The last day, terrible & frightful
Everyone around you will speak
But you will remain silent
However strong your attachment is?
May it be your son or your wife?
The more you look at them
The more you will feel pained
So beware!
Abandon the odd pride
Practice renunciation
Trust truth alone to reach truth.

The Search

The ongoing search
Of a lost child is on
Searching for the destination
In the city of over crowdedness
Places all strange
Some known, some unknown faces,
Nothing appeals, nothing comforts
The emptiness within is widening.
The scare of life and death terrifies
The child closes the eyes
He stops the hunt, and
In stillness he finds
His father waiting for him
More desperate for him, than he himself
To embrace him, to love him
To take him home.
The search is complete.

The Living Church

Church,
A place of testimony
Where one stands
In all honesty to face the truth.
But
The fact is otherwise
Where one stands live in flesh
The body is the true spot of church.
To say nothing but the truth
To think nothing but the truth
To hear nothing but the truth
For
On the Day of Judgment
It is the living heart with truth
A real witness of the testimony.
So, my mind!
Open ears of my heart
Open eyes of my heart
To listen to the truth
And sustain the truth.

Life and Death

The light that vanishes,
The life that is extinguished,
Shall not go beyond the graves,
For it was never ever born,
Nor did it fade.
It is the very source of fundamental living.
We live in deeds, not in years.
For time can never be imprinted on the sands,
That is trodden by the feet of death.
The deeds live there after in memoirs,
So the souls too live in memoirs of life.
Who says souls die?
They never die.
They live with you,
They live in heart beats,
They live in the throbs,
They live, for they never die,
They only re-unite with life.
Death is a reunion
To refresh life that has been lived
It is a steppingstone to a new life
It is a mortal image of those that live
For only they die who live.
Bodies die, souls live
Come they may, but go they must,
The real life starts,
Where death embraces life,
To re-unite with a new life.

Unheard Melody

Nature is so beautifully singing
The unheard tunes, and is whispering
Something more beautiful
Than we have ever heard
More musical than the creations melody
Surpassing the echoing sounds of
All keys of musical instruments
The best tune ever played
Is the one which the heart beats
As it play on the drums of destiny.

A new concept of life

Yes, life is a teacher
A guide to be followed
That teaches us a new lesson
At this hour of new sunrise
With a New Concept of Humanity
To love self, others, and each other
With a passion of Oneness
In a selfless way, to share
The only thing you have
The gift of love, with a loving heart
The gift bestowed on each one by God
The Creator, the caretaker, the destroyer
By his own sweet will, to make us realize
That you and me can't do
What he can do, and
To realize the value of being loved by Him
Him, who never leaves anyone isolated
Does not judge anyone by caste, creed, color
But as a pure form of Love in his own image
Being with each one at us at all times
As a helping hand, for us to realize and believe
The utmost source of faith
That never left us alone in times of need
Rendering his extended hand to humanity
To live, to breathe, to flourish to be a Good Human.

A process of recycling

Nature is now going through
A process of recycling
Of flora, fauna and even the mankind
Under the Sun by the command
Of the creator, the destroyer
To reset the used product, and recreate
The new Brand of all products after recycling
When the world is reset
With new fresh fragrance all around
The blue sky, the whirling winds
The churning water by the shore
To bring freshness in the breaths
Where the viewpoint of seeing
Will be believing the new aura
With different promises of retaining
The identity of all humans
The flower gardens, the ducks by the pond,
The fishes in water, the dolphins by waters deep
Will all greet each other with smiles
Shall be unable to see and recognize
Faces and facts that will be unveiled
As the used masks, are to be destroyed
To inhale and exhale open heartedly
The fresh fragrant flowers of the new season
That bloom from the fresh soil of Mother Earth
From of the new seeds, sprouts and flowers
To nourish the growth of the Plantations.

A new reset of the creation

As it reflects the turbulent past
The hardships of the sinking ship
With modern high-class technology
With possibility to take man to Moon
But before the dawn
Comes the downfall of the
All That Remains significantly
The rise turns to a fall
By the forceful gravity of nature
To balance the new life
That survives after death
To live with a new start
A new reset of the creation
In the world of Wonders
That is all Mighty father's creation

Nature is singing

Nature is singing
The unheard tunes so beautifully
And is whispering
Something more beautiful
Than we have ever heard before
More musical than the compositions
Created by the keys of musical instruments
The best tune is now echoing
The one which only the heart beats can play
On the drums of destiny.

Wants and Wishes

Our wants are always far more
Than our needs
Our wishes have sown innumerable seeds
In the soil of our heart's core
Now waiting for them to sprout
The more we reap,
Much more we sow before that
And now with this state of mind
Where our liberty is caged
We feel dejected and defeated by our own wishes
As the truth has unveiled itself that
We need only what we consume
Have lot more to let go,
As it helps to share and serve.

Today & Tomorrow

What was yesterday is bygone today
Tomorrow is still unknown today
The forecast is reversed:
It is for the past, not future.
Yesterday's future is today,
Today is known and certain
Today's future is tomorrow,
Tomorrow is unknown and uncertain.
Do we have to know our future?
The source makes the decisions
To design our destiny,
Unfolding the uncertainty
From the womb of certainty
The unknown tomorrow
Shall emerge from the womb of today.

Lead and Follow

You said -
Keep on going in front
I shall follow you
Truly enough when I move ahead
I realize the essence of the truth
That I am life and you are death.

Thirst

My mind is a sandy particle
With unquenched thirst
It wanders in search of a drop
Like the *papeeha*
That seeks the first drop of rain
Awaiting all its life till it attains
As the first drop satisfies the *Papeeha* *
Similarly my mind is in search of
The unseen waterfall from eternity
To quench my thirst of births.

(papeeha = Pied Crested Cukoo)

Memories

The library of my heart
Has a collection of old books
With Soiled old papers
With some old shabby scribbles on them
No more readable or understandable
Lost in the bygone gestures of understanding
Beyond the capacity of perception
But
These clips hang on to the walls of my memory
Surprisingly with a sense of receptivity
They are seen and read
Through the lens of memory.

They are glued to the walls of my heart
And cannot be erased, as do
Dust particles from air get glued to
The mirror of memory
That cannot be wiped out, but
Can be unfolded and reviewed with time
As a flash of lightening
When the heart longs to be in the
Companionship of the past
To relate and relish in present
The evergreen memory land of the past.

This moment

Between yesterday and tomorrow
Is my today the prime time of my life
At this moment I realize that
Between the moments of
My past and my future
I still have more precious gifts to enjoy
And relish the fruits of the reality
That sustains the Life and death
That I am not the one who does anything
Someone in me does
I'm not the one who listens
Someone else in me takes the privilege to listen
I am not the one who is able to live life
Someone else lives in me to cherish life
I just die daily to keep myself living.

The Will

On her death bed
She was still in her senses
To know, to understand
The play that was played
Awaiting her death.
But, before that
She was to sign the will
Spread in front of her
With her own sweet will.
The will in front of her
Had choices of everyone and their wishes
To possess what she was to leave behind for them
Just forgetting what she needed, and
Ignoring what she wished for.
It was necessary to sign the blank papers
Below the name typed in black-and-white
Before it was late, she wrote a few words and signed
"Today you are the rulers
Tomorrow you will be governed
At this very place, a new history will be written
Tomorrow your successors will sign themselves,
Without acknowledging your wants and wishes
Where I am signing today."

The Key

If you think you shall stem me
With the shackles of your sweet selfish love
You are mistaken
Don't ever feel the comfort
That you have trapped me in the clutches,
Snatched away my freedom,
It is your idiocy
I am not so foolish to pledge my freedom
For the majestic splendor of your prison
It is true
I have closed the doors of my freedom behind me
But
Still have the key that unlocks the door.
It is long since I have not used it,
Undoubtedly it has rusted a bit
But it is the same key,
And I am very much sure
'The key that locks the lock
Also unlocks it.'

The mirror and me

The mirror grown with me
Is as aged as I am, yet
Knows well how to perform consistently
Patiently with me at every step of my life's journey
With a graceful smile
But lately the wear and tear of usage
Has formed layers of smoky dust around it
However much I try to freshen it up
Yet, I have to see my dusty face
With more wrinkles on my forehead and chin
With its dusty eyes
Neither has he changed
Nor me.

Foundation

The foundation of relationships
If laid on comfort
Tends to be crippled
If established on the convenience of economy
They happen to wreck on the rocks of greed
If based on the foundational fulfillment
Then contentment enriches life
With all the wealths of the world.

The power of unseen

The combat is Ongoing
The power of unseen overrides
What the eyes see
In this atmosphere of uncertainty
The creative power is empowered
By the destructive element
The hugs and kisses are a bygone legacy
The underlying fear of embracing
The loved ones keep the distancing
We see, we hear, we witness
The departing silent cries
The seen and the unseen
Are friend and foe facing each other
Living as contemporaries under
The silent destructive canopy of the ERA
The silent killer chokes
The breaths of hearts in the vibrant body
To install the stillness silently
It is not a choice of freewill
But the freewill of living
That is snatched from the hands of LIFE
To be grounded lifeless in the ground.

Images (Micro Poems)

Life and death are friends,
Death follows life
Life dies with death

The flight of thoughts,
Is limitless,
But breaths have one.

The rays of sunshine
Penetrate through openings
That let them in.

Reality survives,
All dreams come to an end
When I awake.

Ideas when implemented
Reflect to show
The mind as a weapon.

Illusions are like dreams
Make no difference to the mind
As only the mind thinks.
The doors of my heart
Are open to joys and sorrows
With a sign "welcome".

Man is defined
Not by intelligence but acts
That are human.

Storms cannot destroy me
For, I am not a tall palm
I am a tender, humble, flexible bush.

A Friend is a torch
That shows the path to another
On a dark cloudy day.

A streak of light
Penetrates from the darkest cloud,
To absorb all darkness.

Life is born to live
But death chases it
Till it dies.

The doors of my heart
Are open to the sorrows
That bloom to be my joys.

Beauty lies in the hearts
As seen by the seeker
Who captivates it in his own heart.

We have to open
The mind to truth
To cultivate the truth.

Passions are intruders
That robs the truth
That is basis of living

The product of pain
Is definitely pleasure

The fruit of patience.

The dove so beautiful
Is in the prison of love
Though woven from silk.

Thoughts of desperation
Heard inaudible soft velvet whispers
Diffusing in soul's breathless desire.

Heart of hearts
Prevails the truth
Unhidden from self

If The rays of the sun
Pierce through the clouds
To reach the ground

Close your eyes
See the boundary
Beyond it.

Between the lines
Are lines that really go
Unread all the time.
As the setting sun
Melts below the horizon
Stars applaud her now.

Experts' Views

Poetry of Hope

Poetry knows no boundaries -- of race, gender or geography. The poetry in the "Ringing Radiance" breaks another bar, that is the bar of time. The transcendental message that is the essence of this collection is the message that existed in human heart long before you and I were born and is going to last as long as the thinking species exists anywhere.

The poetry, the words, meaning, and the spirit of "Ringing Radiance" points to the message of life, the message of knowing ourselves. While reading "Ringing Radiance" the reader interviews self. The poetry interrogates, and at the same time it reviews in retrospect. For example, 'The mirror and me' beautifully describes the mirror that reflects us, the one that knows us inside and out. The other thing it tells us is about the common source, the trinity - the creator, the preserver, and the destroyer. Following lines beautifully relay the lines of 'Sukh duhkhe same krtvaa' from the Bhagvadgita:

Life is born to live
But death chases it
Till it dies.

The doors of my heart
Are open to the sorrows
That bloom to be my joys.

Same 'Bhagvadgita' reminds us about our immortality through 'Na Hanyate Hanyamane Sharire'. So do the poems in this collection by showing us the ray of hope. These poems brings forward the ancient wisdom of the sages of the Vedas. We are reassured that the world existed before our mortal body took form, and the same will continue way beyond the the point that is generally considered the end. Devi ji in her poems talks about uncovering the truth in a way that reminds us the visionaries of Ishopanishada:

The rays of the sun
Pierce through the clouds
To reach the ground

or the eternal truth of 'Brahm Satyam Jagat Mithya' through the following lines

Reality survives,
All dreams come to an end
When I awake

The poems cover a wide variety of subjects we all experience (or will realize at some point of time). While 'This moment' tells something that seem obvious, though not for most of us, the next poem 'The will' sets up a completely different stage.

Some of these poems take a deep dive into spirituality while some provide us basic advice to deal with the issues coming as a package deal with our day-to-day life. Overall, this collection reminds us of 'Atmavat Sarva Bhuteshu' that means everybody is ours, everyone is part of the same source, each soul essentially lives within the space created by the super soul that created us forever free as depicted in the following lines from suitably titled poem 'The Key':

It is true
I have closed the doors of my freedom behind me
But
Still have the key that unlocks the door.
It is long since I have not used it,
Undoubtedly it has rusted a bit
But it is the same key,
And I am very much sure
'The key that locks the lock

Also unlocks it.'

These poems bring us to the state of consciousness where we can truly experience the radiance ringing inside, justifying the title of the book. We as readers, not only hear it, see it, we actually go beyond experiencing it - we become one with it.

Anurag Sharma 'Setu'
Pittsburgh, USA

The Affirming Poetics of Devi Nangrani in the time of pandemic---and beyond

Each singing what belongs to him or her and to none else.
---Walt Whitman

In "I hear America Singing", Walt Whitman celebrates the land, labour and their songs and the joy of being alive in a democracy that promises equality, equity, justice and happiness as an evolved society; a dream society created by the collective work force and their generational aspirations towards a livable and better civilization; and their communal labour producing resultant songs of happiness, the "varied carols" that the poet can hear across America.

For great poets, that is the enduring literary project---celebrating nations and peoples, via their works of high quality, morality and humanism---works rooted in the soil, community and self---as realized vehicle or mode of perecption.

Multi-lingual and prolific author Devi Nangrani, in her latest collection of poetry *Ringing Radiance*, celebrates life in all its moods, colours and sounds, like every serious-minded writer and artist.

Like Whitman, this Indian-American poet, too, talks of the land and joys of singing in such a liberating cultural geography; her voice representing an entire country in its cadence and variety, a kind of spiritual symphony where body-soul, micro-macro, this-that worlds collapse into a fresh entity, thus the self becoming the collective, the poetic voice expressing the multiple voices:

I am the singing melody of my Land
That gently tunes in rhythm

Wrapping me in her essence.
My thoughts dance in tune
With the melody of my heartbeat
In the Canopy of fragrance
They dance as daisies in my memory
Growing with me where I stand
Sometimes longer, at times shorter
But never have I felt without the Source.
(From: "The music of my heart")

What is this source?
Here, in her inspiring words, it gets defined aptly:

On
The wings of thought,
I, rise high and high
To See the glory of nature
In

Pleasure and paradise,
In pool of pain and misery

("The Source")

Nature, Godhood, self, self- realization, among other interweaving threads, constitute the major patterns that bind together this 60-poem volume of her deep meditation on what it means to be a human and sentient being, in a post-industrial culture This inquiry leads to singular epiphanies.

Take a close look:

I prostrate unto Thee
One who hath rendered peace unto me.

In my heart, thy compassionate voice is heard,
Oh Lord! None excels you in this world.

Unaware of you from time of my birth,
I was singing the glory of Hari, Hara and Brahma:

Only now I have realized that you are Effulgence,
That you are the "Lord of Lords"

And the Ringing Radiance

("Ringing Radiance")

This is a rich and complex poetic landscape that evokes the physical and metaphysical, mystic and real, romantic and reflective, source and peripheral, most competently in a language understood by heart--- a book of songs that remains affirmative, faith-centred and optimistic in its overall vision and delicately wrought execution, for an audience recovering from a deadly pandemic and moving beyond despair and death.

Glimpses of the seen and unseen deftly captured by a senior writer and thinker.

Words that reveal the truths behind the phenomena, otherwise missed by an ordinary mind.

Catch them---the fleeting moments, explained and defined by a blessed eye.

They will lead to further journeys of self-evolution, along better-illuminated pathways of words and melodies.

Sunil Sharma,
Editor, Setu
Mumbai, India

In Quest ...

Devi Nangrani's poems are the expressions of genuinely and intensely experienced love, devotion and mystic relationship with the Divinity. She can hear the sound of silence even in the midst of the 'Whirlpool of roaring waters' the din and turmoil of worldly existence. She is aware of the 'taste of love' that takes hold of life, makes one give up freedom and accept its bondages. She is also aware that the soul will attain true freedom only after breaking away from the cage of this body, flying as a free bird. After going through her representative poems one feels convinced that the poet is no common human being but a sprit in quest of eternal peace. She intends to fly like a free bird singing on the perch in the woods of sanctuary 'To fulfill the goal of life'.

She exhorts her soul to awake, radiate and create its own powerhouse of radiance. Devi has poignant perception of the minutest working of the mind,

"When a single Thought precedes yet another clashes,
cracks breaks leaving the turmoil of mind still to survive."

Her faith in divinity is firm; hence, there is spontaneity in her feeling and expressions. The experiences recorded in most of her poems are those of a keen and sensitive observer. Some of the poems reveal her inner silence which slowly and gradually ravishes the reader of a world of beauty and ecstasy.

In a world which is plagued by cut-throat competition materialistic pursuit, Devi's poetry breathes an air of pure divinity and rectitude.

Dr. Lakhbir Kaur
Director,
Guru Harkishan High school & Junior College of Commerce
North Av Road, Khardanda,
Santacruz W, Mumbai-400054

On this journey of Inner Adventure

To travel with Devi Nangrani is nothing but sheer pleasure, joining her on this journey, in search of self and Him. There are oasis which invite and allure, but a true seeker though diverted to the perishable beauties and temporary achievements awakens back on the right path, because, the ultimate destination is to surrender oneself at His Lotus Feet to merge with Him.

The poetess here beautifully portrays the fallacies like misery, mental turbulences as a seeker in simple, pictorial and gripping language. 'Request to the mind' is a wonderful poem. Persuing the 'Songs of the heart' that have to be sung.

Within the core
We find the link of silence
From it sprout the buds of true spirit
That lead us to the road of silence
Help us discover the lost city.

I wish Devi all the best for this book, and I am sure readers will find the same yearning in their hearts when they start their journey to find 'The lost city'.

May we all share the same happiness as we join here on this journey.

Dr. Sangeeta Sahajwani
H.O.D, Dept of Hindi, R. D. National College,
Bandra, Mumbai-400050

A Journey from Birth to Death and Beyond

"Within me is an island
Hidden from the sea of my body.
There I shed a tear
Hidden from the eye of the heart'. -'Journey'

Yes like perhaps in each one of us, there is an island in Devi Nangrani's heart and mind, hidden away even from the eyes of the heart, even from - our lifelong companion - our physical body and she visits that island occasionally to shed a tear, to 'Listen to her heart Beat', but she does not dwell there for longer period because she is not a recluse, or and escapist. She may be alone sometimes but she is never lonely. She comes away to the shore, to the main land, the solid earth to her kith and kin, to her social concern and commitments. But how does she manage to cross the stormy, turbulant sea that surrounds the sea island?

The poems in her anthology 'Journey' give answers to these questions. She has the support of faith':

'If
You see with eyes of faith
The unseen world within you
Opens the gates for you to a new world.'

But at the very outset writer knows that inspite of the helplessness of the mind, inspite of the 'Mirage' like qualities of life, you have to 'Be your own friend' and have faith and courage so that you can listen to the music of your heart and can feel 'the Spirit' within you. Devi Nangrani has penned down these simple, serene poems as one would note down the slow, silent, waves of thoughts passing through our heart and mind.

Devi Nangrani is writer who has command over Hindi and English beside her mother tongue Sindhi and has been expressing her emotions and feelings through these languages. I heartily congratulate her for this poetic journey through birth, death and beyond.

Dr. Rajam Natarajan Pillai
Editor: 'Kutubnuma' Hindi Quarterly
'Ramkunj'. R.K. Vaidya Rd, Dadar (W)
Mumbai 400 028, Mob: 9820229565

On the shore of Sand and Pebbles

In search of self: is a beautiful poem, The expression in the poetry as I read here your thoughts and smooth writings are beautiful. There is no doubt that you are a great poet and thinker, the world needs inspiration to move positively. I hope more people will have deep appreciation for the truth that is inducted in them from the moment of creation. Wisdom and philosophy are more nourishing to life than protein and carbohydrate for the body. I hope the day will dawn when sophisticated men relinquish ego, false pride, vanity, greed and wear a clean shawl, touching the sand and pebbles and experience the presence of god.

Shri Jaswant Behari
Boloji.com

Author's Bio-Data

Devi Nangrani

Born before partition in Karachi (Bharat then), Devi Nangrani been teaching and learning in the school of Life. She writes Prose, poetry, reviews, articles on women issues, ghazals, and has translated 12 books of stories of writers of Sindh and Hind from Sindhi to Hindi Language.

Education: B.A: Early Childhood from NJCU, Mathematics Teachers Training in India and NJ, Profession: Teacher, NJ (now retired)

Languages: Mother Tongue - Sindhi, Hindi, Gurmukhi, Urdu, Telugu, Marathi, English, Spanish.

PUBLISHED BOOKS:

Sindhi Books:

Gam Bhinal Khushi (Ghazal-2007), Ud Ja Panchi (Bhajan-2007), Aas Ki Shamma (Ghazal-2008), Sindh ki Jaayi (Karachi Academy-2009), Ghazal (Ghazal-2012), Maan Khinjo Naahiyaan (Story-2016), Siju Lahan Baid (story-2018), Amma chayo ho (Poetry-2019), Lafzi Libaas (Book Reviews-2020), Nazaqat Rishatan Ji (Kathas-2020)

Hindi books:

Charage-Dil (Ghazal-2007), Dil Se Dil Tak (Ghazal-2008), Lau Dard-E-Dil ki (Ghazal-2008), Bhajan Mahima (Bhajan-2012), Aisa Bhi hota Hai (Story -2016), Sahan-E-Dil (Ghazal-2017), Ganga Nirantar Bahti Rahi (Laghukatha-2017), Maan ne Kaha tha (poetry-2017), Jung Zari hai (story-2018), Qalam ke Vividh Roop (Reviews-2018), Bahte pani mein Daraein(sansmaran-2019) Jeevan ke pahalu (Inspirational-2019), Parchaaiyon ka Jungal (story-2019), Dohavali-Haiku (2020)

Translation from Hindi to Sindhi:

Baarish ki Dua (story-2012), Apni Dharti (story-2013), Roohani Rooh ke pathik (Poetry-2014), Barf ki Garmaish (short stories-2014), Aamne-Saamne (Poetry-2016), Ankh Ye Dhanya Hai (Narendra Modi Poetry-2017), Chauthi Koot (Story-SAcademy Publication-2018),

Translation from Sindhi to Hindi:

Aur main Badi Ho Gai (Story-2012), 15 Sindhi Kahanyaan (Story-2014), Sindhi Kahaniyaan (Story-2014), Sarhadon ki kahaniyaan (Story-2015), Kavya Saundary (Poetry -

2015), Apne Hi Ghar mein (Story-2016), Dard Ki Ek Gatha (Story -2016), Ek Thaka Hua Sach (Attiya Dawood Poetry-2016), Aamne-saamne-Poetry-(2016) Vibhajan ki Trasadi (Partition kahani -2017) Prant Prant Ki kahaniyaan (Multilingual stories-2019),

English Book and other translations:

The Journey (English Poetry-2009)

Safar zindagi (Tr. of Journey in Hindi & Sindhi By: Dhruv Tanvani -2016)

Sindhi Katha (Marathi Tr. stories By Dr. Vidhya Chitko-2016)

Rumi Masanavi: (Translation from English to Hindi & Sindhi -2020)

After the Sunset (English Stories-Tr. Ram Daryani-Press)

Aisa bhi hota hai (Punjabi stories-Tr. Jagdish Kulrian)

Parchhiyon ka jungal (Urdu kahani-Tr-Amir Siddique)

Ringing Radiance-: (English -Poetry)

Awards and recognitions:

New York, New Jersey, Oslo, Chennai, Raipur, Jodhpur, Delhi, Lucknow, Dharwaad-Karnataka, Kolkota, Goa, Keral, Sagar NCPSL, different national and international Academies.

Kavya mani samman-Proclamation Honour Award-Mayor NJ-2008, Kavya Ratna- and Kavya Mani-Vidhyadhaam-& Siskshayatan 2008, Sarv Bharateey Bhasha Samman-Maharashtra Academy-2008, Hindi Sahitya Sevi Samman Bharateey Norwegian Forum-OSLO-2011, Sahitya Setu Samman-Tamilnadu Hindi Academy-2013, Sayyad Meer Ali Meer Pusruskaar-MP-2013, AMRITA Preetham Literary National Award-2014, Hindi Sevi Samman-Keral-2015, Pravasi Sahitykaar Samman-

Sagar-2017. Awards from NCPSL-2007, Maharashtra Rajya Sindhi Sahitya Academy-2019.

Translated stories from SINDHI to HINDI now in Text & Voice can be heard at:

https://nangranidevi.blogspot.com/

Contact: dnangrani@gmail.com

About Setu Publications

Setu Publications is an extension of Pittsburgh based Setu bilingual journal. It operates on a no-profit-no-loss basis.

The idea is to provide serious literary content in book-form to the reading community. For any query, write in, please: setuedit@gmail.com, with the subject line: Book Publication.

Proud to present the works by our distinguished writers below. Click on images to know more about each book.

The small press aims to serve those authors interested in getting published in USA by a house known for quality. The books published by Setu are made available worldwide on Amazon. Editorial consultations with the authors, at every stage of production of print-ready texts, and, selection of covers and cover designs, are done regularly by our experienced team members. Due to the limited availability of human resources, the editing of the manuscripts is not offered currently, though due care is taken to ensure quality. The post-production publicity and literary reviews are the sole responsibilities of the concerned authors only.

We respect all languages, but due to some limitations beyond our control, the books in Indian languages can be published only in Kindle eBook format and not in hardbound or paperbacks generally.

Setu Bilingual monthly journal is available online at the following link:
https://www.setumag.com/p/setu-home.html

With Setu, you are in a good company.

Minotaur, A Dark Tale
Sunil Sharma

The Body of Memories
(Lopamudra Banerjee)

Cross-Stitched Words (Poetry)
Chaitali Sengupta

Ringing Radiance: The Powerhouse
Devi Nangrani

Only and Again (Poetry)
Dustin Pickering

Wanderer (Poetry)
Rajender Krishan Chowdhry

Orange Dawn
John Clark Smith

Women, Nurturing Outlook and Ecology
Sangeeta Sharma

Amma's Gospel And Other Poems
By Rajender Krishan

Solitude And Other Poems*
By Rajender Krishan

English Pronunciation Dictionary
By Amin Rahman

Monsoon Swing And Other Poems
By Lavanya Shah

Ps-Fs :: Sunil Sharma

Paco's Atlas And Other Poems
By John Thieme

India as an IT Superpower
Anurag Sharma

अनुरागी मन कथा संग्रह :: अनुराग शर्मा*

आग से अंतरिक्ष तक :: अजीज राय*

Basic Hindi 2 Workbook :: Sonia Taneja

छोटी सी बात :: अनुराग शर्मा*

She Spoke in Tongues :: Glory Sasikala

Aesthetic Negotiations
Sunil Sharma

Photo Essays - Rajender Krishan

www.ingramcontent.com/pod-product-compliance
Lightning Source LLC
LaVergne TN
LVHW020048110826
845155LV00029B/677

* 9 7 8 1 9 4 7 4 0 3 1 2 3 *